Lullaby

Bayou Lullaby

by Kathi Appelt

pictures by Neil Waldman

·Morrow Junior Books·
New York

petite chérie (puh TEET SHUH ree): my little darling.

pirogue (PEER oh): a small flat-bottomed boat with high sides, usually steered with a pole; it can skim over very shallow water.

To Pat, *ma belle mama*
—K.A.

For Roy Lee,
sometimes my father,
sometimes my son,
always my brother
—N.W.

Rockabye, you bayou gal,
Cattails be a-swishin'
Softly sigh, oh bayou gal,
On a star be wishin'.

Don't you worry, *ma petite,*
Your pirogue's safely moored
Atop the water *chocolat*
Amid the reeds ashore.

Your mama's sittin' by your bed
To tuck you, *bébé* mine,
'tween cotton sheets that smell of sun
From hangin' on the line.

So close your eyes now, drift away
And in the by and by
The king of bullfrogs, King Armand,
Will croon a lullaby.

His silver notes be settlin' down
To soothe the alligators
Now go to sleep, *petite chérie,*
My little sweet potato.

Mosquitoes be a-buzzin'
Round the porch light's yellow glow
And tree frogs add a chorus,
Fais dodo, fais dodo.

Listen.
King Armand be whistlin'
To crawdads 'neath the waves
Crawdads snoozin' in the mud
Of cozy crawdad caves.

Hear the cricket's harmonizin'
To the bullfrog's deep bassoon
And herons tuck their heads
Beneath their wings, beneath the moon.

That moon's a-dancin' in the sky
A-waltzin' 'twixt the stars
And King Armand be hummin' now
His lullaby's last bars.

So snuggle down, my bayou gal,
And dream a bayou dream
Of water driftin' slowly down
To meet the sleepy sea.

It curls around the cypress trees
Whose feet stand deep beneath
The muddy water *chocolat*
Where tadpoles hide and seek.

Shhh . . .
King Armand is quiet now
Too soon the sun will rise
To wake the oysters from their beds
And light the darkened sky.

But till ol' Sol be shinin'
Let the fireflies be your light
And rockabye, you bayou gal,
Oh bayou gal, good night.

The author wishes to gratefully acknowledge Professor Barry Jean Ancelet of the Folk Life Center
at the University of Southwestern Louisiana for his gracious review of this manuscript.

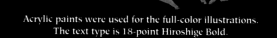

Acrylic paints were used for the full-color illustrations.
The text type is 18-point Hiroshige Bold.

Library of Congress Cataloging-in-Publication Data
Appelt, Kathi.
Bayou lullaby/Kathi Appelt; illustrated by Neil Waldman.
p. cm.
Summary: A colorful good-night poem to a "bayou gal." Includes a glossary with Cajun pronunciation.
ISBN 0-688-12856-4 (trade)—ISBN 0-688-12857-2 (library)
[1. Bayous—Fiction. 2. Cajuns—Fiction. 3. Bedtime—Fiction. 4. Sleep—Fiction. 5. Night—Fiction. 6. Lullabies.
7. Stories in rhyme.] I. Waldman, Neil, ill. II. Title. PZ8.3.A554Bay 1995 [E]—dc20 94-16639 CIP AC